ROCKS
and
MINERALS

Troll Associates

ROCKS
and
MINERALS

by Rae Bains

Illustrated by R. Maccabe

Troll Associates

Library of Congress Cataloging in Publication Data

Bains, Rae.
    Rocks and minerals.

    Summary: Discusses briefly the characteristics and
uses of some common rocks and minerals.
    1. Rocks—Juvenile literature.   2. Mineralogy—
Juvenile literature.   [1. Rocks.   2. Mineralogy]
I. Maccabe, Richard, ill.   II. Title.
QE432.2.B35   1985   552   84-8644
ISBN 0-8167-0186-5 (lib. bdg.)
ISBN 0-8167-0187-3 (pbk.)

Wherever you are on earth, rocks are all around you. There are big rocks, called boulders, and there are small stones and tiny pebbles. The sand on a beach is really millions of tiny grains of rock. Soil contains even smaller pieces of rock. And mud contains very, very small bits of rock mixed with water.

7

Mountains are huge masses of rock that soar into the sky. Deserts are great amounts of tiny rocks that can stretch for miles like vast dry seas. The oceans of the world cover even more rock. Indeed, the earth itself is an enormous ball of rock.

The rocks we can see are part of a thin layer of the earth's surface called the crust. In some places, the crust is only six miles thick. But under this thin crust there is a

special kind of rock, called magma. Magma is a rock that is in a liquid form because it is so hot.

Most of the time we never get to see the magma under the earth's crust. But when a volcano erupts, we can see hot rivers of magma that are pushed up to the earth's surface. Magma that reaches the earth's surface is called lava.

The world's oldest rocks, called igneous rocks, were formed when magma cooled and hardened. There are two groups of igneous rocks, extrusive and intrusive.

In the first group are *extrusive* rocks, which formed when magma erupted from volcanoes. Three examples of extrusive rocks are obsidian, pumice, and basalt.

Obsidian is black and always has sharp edges. American Indians often used obsidian to make arrowheads and knives. Pumice is light gray in color and is so light in weight that it actually floats on water! It is often ground into powder, and used for polishing things. Basalt is dark gray, and is made up of fine grains of minerals. Crushed basalt is often used for building roads.

Unlike extrusive rocks, *intrusive* rocks were formed when magma cooled *below* the earth's surface. The most common intrusive rock is called granite. Granite is light in color. It is a hard, durable rock that is often used for buildings and monuments.

Although granite and other intrusive igneous rocks are formed below the earth's surface, they may be uncovered by natural forces, such as earthquakes, faults, or fractures. Or they may be exposed when the rocks above them are worn away.

When rocks of any kind are worn away, we say that erosion has taken place. Many things cause erosion, such as wind, rain, the movement of a glacier, or the rushing water of a river or a waterfall.

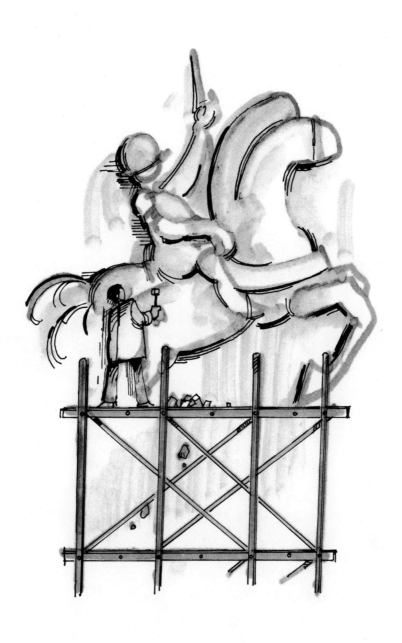

13

When a rock erodes, the bits that come off it are blown or carried to another place, where they are deposited. These bits of rock are known as sediment. Over a long period of time, the layers of sediment build up higher and higher, with the top layers pressing down on the layers below them.

After many, many centuries the layers become a kind of rock called sedimentary rock. Sedimentary rock may contain bits of

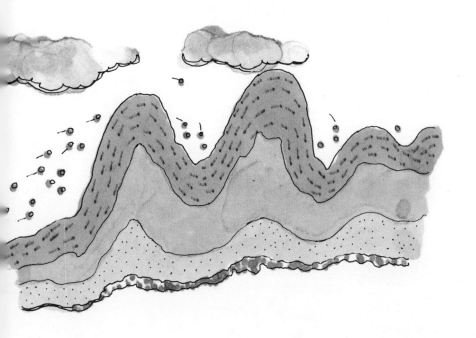

any kind of rock. This is why sedimentary rocks come in so many colors and textures.

Any time you see rock that has layers, you know it is sedimentary rock. If the layers are flat, like those of a layer cake, the oldest layers are on the bottom, and the youngest layers are on the top. But sometimes you see layers of sedimentary rock that are curled or tilted. Then it is hard to tell which are the oldest and youngest layers.

Shale

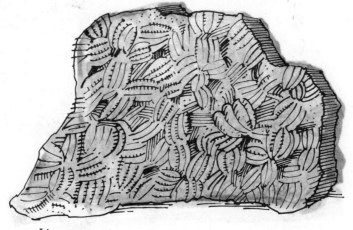

Sandstone

Limestone

The most common sedimentary rock is called shale. Shale is a fairly soft rock, made mostly of tiny bits of mud and clay. Shale is used to make bricks and cement.

Another common sedimentary rock is sandstone. Sandstone, which is mostly grains of sand, can be red, brown, gray, yellow, or white. The color usually comes from the minerals that hold the sand grains together.

A third common sedimentary rock is called limestone. Limestone is made up mostly of a mineral called calcite, which came from the shells of sea animals. Over many thousands of years, layers of these shells built up. Then, for some reason, the water in which the animals lived evaporated. And what was left was limestone.

Chalk is a form of limestone. In England, there are huge chalk deposits called the White Cliffs of Dover. If you look at a piece of Dover chalk under a magnifying glass, you can see the tiny shells that formed it.

Like limestone, other sedimentary rocks may contain fossils. Fossils are the remains of

ancient plants or animals, or the marks left by them. Just as limestone contains shells, coal often contains the fossils of plants that were growing when the coal began to form.

Sandstone and shale also may contain the fossils of ancient plants and animal life. If you see a rock with a fossil, you know that it is probably a sedimentary rock.

Sometimes, as a result of heat or pressure, or a combination of the two, an igneous rock or a sedimentary rock changes into a new type of rock. This new type of rock is called metamorphic rock. The word *metamorphic* comes from the Greek word meaning "to change form."

Heat and pressure cause a chemical change within the rock itself. This chemical change forms new minerals and changes the color, texture, and hardness of the rock. When shale, which is soft, undergoes metamorphosis, it becomes slate, which is hard. Many school chalkboards are made of slate.

When limestone undergoes metamorphosis, it becomes marble. Marble is a
fine-grained rock that can be polished to a
silky smoothness. Often called the most
beautiful rock of all, marble is used for
statues, monuments, and public buildings.

Whether a rock is igneous, sedimentary, or metamorphic, it always contains minerals. A mineral always has the same chemical make-up no matter where it is found. Diamonds, sapphires, emeralds, quartz, feldspar, and garnet are examples of minerals. So are gold, silver, copper, graphite, mica, and sulfur.

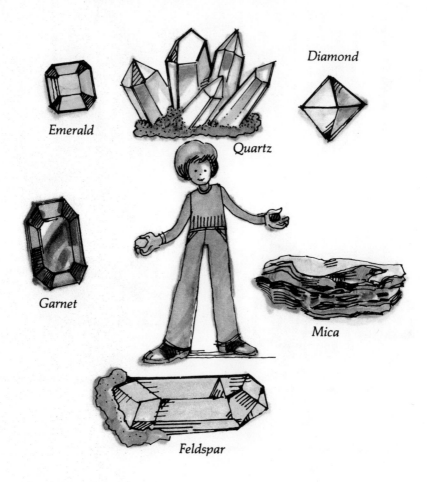

Emerald

Quartz

Diamond

Garnet

Mica

Feldspar

The atoms of a mineral are grouped together in such a way as to form solid units called crystals. Minerals can be identified by the shape of their crystals, their hardness, their color, and how much they shine.

The shape of the crystals determines how the mineral cleaves, or splits. The mineral called halite, which is common salt, cleaves into small cubes with straight sides. Mica, another mineral, splits into very thin flakes. A diamond may split into a pyramid shape. But some minerals, including quartz and gold, do not cleave. They do not split apart cleanly. Instead, they may break into odd-shaped pieces.

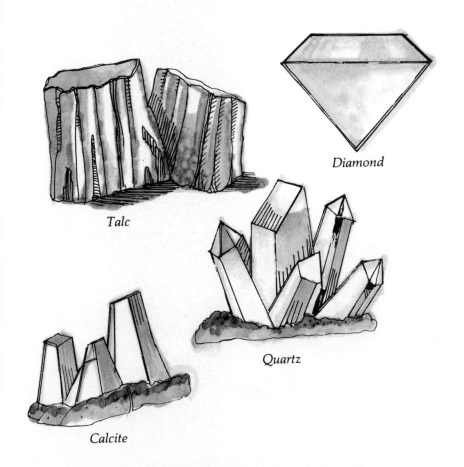

Diamond

Talc

Quartz

Calcite

The scale of hardness for minerals goes from one to ten. Talc, which is very soft and is used for talcum powder, has a hardness of one. Calcite has a hardness of three and can be scratched by a copper penny. Quartz has a hardness of seven and can scratch glass. Diamond, the hardest natural substance on earth, can scratch all other natural substances. It has a hardness of ten.

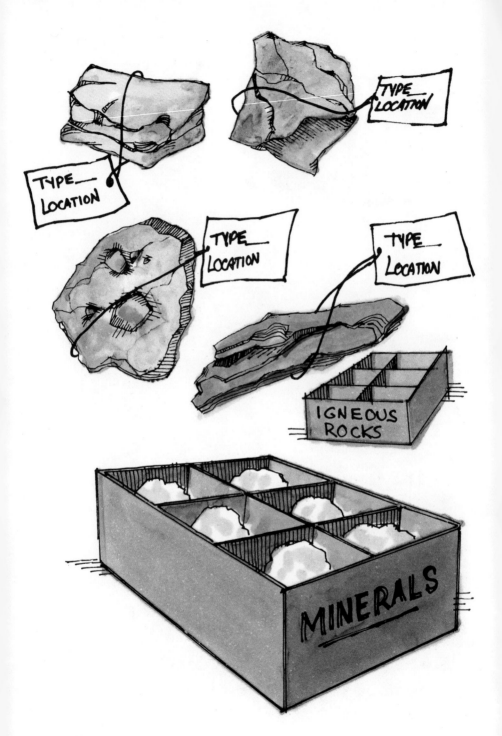

TYPE____
LOCATION

TYPE____
LOCATION

TYPE____
LOCATION

TYPE____
LOCATION

IGNEOUS
ROCKS

MINERALS

The color of a mineral and its luster, which is how much it shines, can also be used to identify it. And if a mineral leaves a streak on a streak plate, such as the back of a tile, the color of the streak may also be a clue to what kind of mineral it is. There are other kinds of tests that can be made on minerals, but they require special scientific equipment.

Many people collect different kinds of rocks and minerals. They identify each sample they have collected and organize the samples into displays. They have discovered that the world of rocks and minerals is a fascinating one.

It's fun to collect rocks. And it's easy to get started collecting them. Because no matter where you are on earth, rocks are all around you!